The Harvest
A Simple, Step by Step Strategy for Making $300 per Week Trading the Foreign Exchange

By Cecil Selkirk

Prologue

Most people believe that it is our natural right as human beings to benefit from our hard work. In days past, farmers would till the soil, sew the seed, wait for rain, weed and tend their crops and then late in the fall when the time was just right, harvest what was hopefully a bountiful crop.

Believe it or not the Foreign Exchange, as with any market, can operate the same way. If we prepare correctly, sew properly, tend our crops and then harvest in a timely fashion, every week we can enjoy a small bounty of what has become an almost four trillion dollar a day currency market.

First though, a few words about me. Until a few years ago I was not a professional trader at all; in fact, I used to be an Economics professor at a small community college. For years I helped students learn how economies function. But like a lot of small colleges during the Great Recession of 2008 I was laid off, and as I struggled to make my house payment, feed and clothe my children and generally try to live a full and happy life I realized that I would need to somehow do it in an economy where there were no jobs available. And even though the economy started to turn around in 2009 and 2010, a "jobless recovery" as they called it, this didn't help me as I scrambled to pay the bills. Finally, a former colleague of mine suggested I try trading the Forex, "it's almost like gambling," she said, "but you can fix the odds in your favor." Over the course of three years I struggled, trying every method, every trading robot and indicator I could find until I developed this simple method of taking not always what you want from the market, but what you need. It was then that I began to make money, and it is only now that I've decided to share my method with others.

So please understand the trading methodology described in this book was first developed from my own necessity, but now it is meant to benefit those most in need, people like you.

Contents

Chapter One: Preparing the Soil

Everything in this book has been written in the simplest content possible for two reasons. The first reason is because one of the most important things you need to know about trading is that you have to keep things simple. In the old days farmers kept things as simple as possible because that was all they could afford, for that reason things were always made to be easy to understand. Back in the old days people didn't have smart phones and desktop computers but instead they used the best technology they had, and a lot of times that was just a copy of the Farmer's Almanac, a plow, a mule, and some pretty good guesswork. And that worked just fine most of the time.

The second reason things have been kept as simple as possible is because I want you to learn, I want you to stretch your imagination, I want you to test and experiment and I want you to figure things out on your own. I will give you all the basics, but when the job is finally complete and you are making three hundred dollars per week trading on the foreign exchange, you really will have figured it all out on your own and you won't need me anymore. That being said, I won't abandon you, because at the back of this book in the Afterword I will put my personal email address, and you can send me any questions you have and I will make every effort to answer your questions as best I can, but remember it wasn't too long ago I was right where you are, just starting out.

So let's talk about you for a moment. It's important we talk about you because in order for you to trade successfully your mind has to be in the right place. This is lesson number one, the importance of fear and greed. Fear and greed is what drives the equity markets, it's what drive the Forex. In order for you to be successful you must learn to control these emotions, because these emotions are what will get you out of a trade too early, or too late. It will mean the difference between having made your three hundred dollars per week or losing part of your trading capital, your seed money, which you must guard at all costs. So please, when you trade, try to be mindful of your emotions, breathe deep, be patient, and meditate on your actions and don't lose control when you trade-it can mean the difference between winning and losing. A little patience helps too; it will help you to stay in control during a live trade.

For our purposes, preparing the soil means setting up your trading platform. In order to do this you will obviously need a computer, I like to trade with a desktop PC but you can use a laptop just as easily. Your network connection is important too. It must be fast and reliable. I do not recommend a dial up connection; in order to properly trade you will sometimes need to get in and out of a trade fast and dial up will not always get the job done. Next, I want you to go to any one of the major Forex dealers; FXDD, FXCM, or IBFX and download their MT4 platform onto your computer. I prefer IBFX, not because I get some special kickback or anything like that but only because you can easily download their MT4 platform and it's easy to open a demo account with IBFX. Some of the other companies want all your private billing information up front and their demo accounts expire after just thirty days but with IBFX you can open unlimited demo accounts for free.

Once you've done downloaded MT4 and opened it up you'll notice it will have the "four majors" shown as open charts on your trading platform. That is to say the currency pairs; EURUSD, GBPUSD, USDJPY and USDCHF. We are not interested in having all four of these pairs open so close them all immediately. We want to start with a fresh slate. I primarily trade AUDUSD or EURUSD. As of this writing I trade exclusively AUDUSD, I only trade this one pair. The reason I trade this pair is because generally speaking it moves the way it's supposed to. It lands on all the Fibonacci retracements it's supposed to and generally speaking lands on all the support and resistance lines it supposed to land on. Remember, in all actuality the market is not supposed to do anything predictable, the market is wild and free and will do and go wherever it wants, but in our world, with this trading methodology I am about to teach you, AUDUSD seems to work best and is fairly predictable. EURUSD will work too, but with all that is happening with the sovereign debt crisis and the problems with Greece possibly defaulting the EURUSD has become a very unpredictable "crop" to trade.

Now that you have MT4 downloaded I want you to open a AUDUSD chart, by default it should open as a H1 or hourly chart, that's fine, leave it as it is. What you will see is a grid and a bunch of tiny bars. This is not what we want to look at when we trade so I am going to teach you how to clean up this raw chart to make it readable. Follow my instructions carefully:

1) Right click on the chart; this will open a "Properties" box. Click on the "Common" tab.

2) First unclick any boxes that are clicked. Now click these boxes only: Chart shift, Chart Autoscroll, Candlesticks, Show OHLC. Now Click "OK" and the Properties box will close.

3) Now right click on the chart again. Click on "Zoom In" twice. This will enhance the green bars against a black background.

4) Right click on the chart again. Scroll down to "Template" and move the cursor to the very top where it says "Save Template," I want you to save the template. Please name the template "Standard H1."

5) Repeat this same process three times except I want you to make Standard templates for these time frames: M15, H1, H4 and D1. It's easy to change the time frames using the toolbar on top, just click on the time frame you want and it will automatically change. Name the templates:

"Standard M15," "Standard H1," "Standard H4," and "Standard D1."

When you are finished with this you will have four Standard templates ready to fill with the indicators we need. Here is what your Standard M15 template will look like:

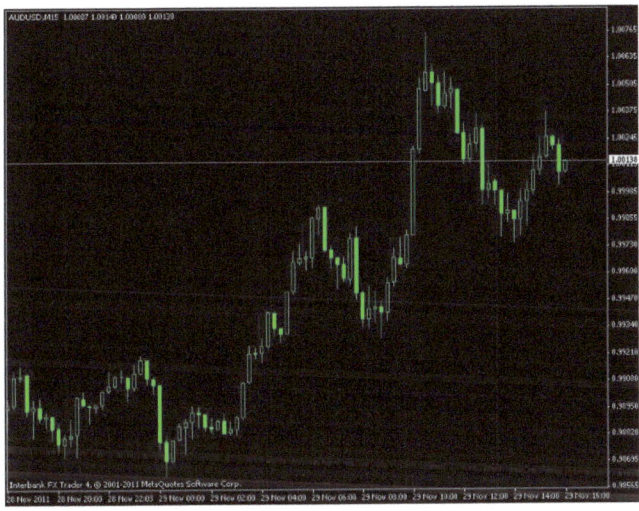

Now that the Standard templates are ready we will need to add the indicators that we will be using to read our charts. Start with your Standard M15 chart. Click on the yellow star at the top left hand corner of the MT4 platform, this will open up a white tool bar on the left side of the screen. I want you to click on Indicators. There are a myriad of indicators that one can use to trade but for our method we only need a few simple, reliable ones. The first one I want you to double click on is the fourth one down and is called Average Directional Movement or ADX for short. Double click on this and a box will open up on the screen. Here is how I want you to set it up:

1)   Click on "Parameters." "Period" should read 14, "Apply to" should read "Close" and "Style" should be Lime.

2)   Next click on colors. I want you to change them. "+DI" should be "Blue" and "-DI" should be "Red." The line choices next to each should be solid, thin lines, not the dotted line that it is showing.

3)   Now click on "Levels" I want you to add two levels only, 20 and 25.

4)   Don't worry about the final tab, "Visualization." "All Timeframes" and "Show in the Data Window" should be clicked. The other boxes stay empty by default.

      Now click "OK" in the bottom of the window and what you will see is the ADX indicator at the bottom of the chart. ADX should have three lines all intersecting at what appear to crazy places. The lines should be Lime green, Red and Blue. I want you to study the Lime green line, this is called the ADX main line, notice that when the line goes up, the bars on the chart also go up,

and notice when the line "snaps" or suddenly breaks downward after climbing at a steep angle that the bars will flat line-we call this ranging. This is when price is neither going up or down but ranges in a very tight pattern, neither rising nor falling any significant amount. Also, when the Blue line is going up, price is rising, the bars on the chart will rise, when the Red line starts to rise, then price starts to drop, or the bars on the chart start to move downward. Here is what your Standard M15 with ADX template will look like:

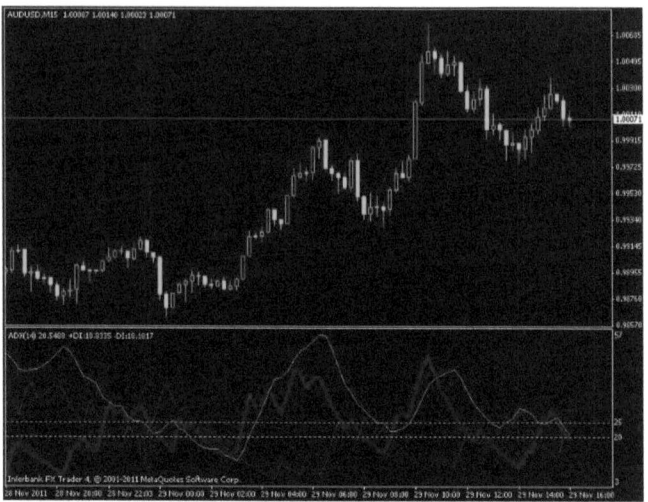

Here are some other important things to know about ADX:

1)   When all three lines are below 20 or 25 then price is ranging, its means the market is essentially resting for the moment, it's going neither up nor down. When these lines start to rise above 20-25 is when it becomes important. That's when price is starting to rise, once either of these lines breaks 30 then prices is really on the move. I have an indicator that will send you an email alert when any of these lines moves above these

levels, but I'll tell you more about that in the Afterword. Its can help you by giving you a signal that price is moving while you're sleeping, since most of Forex price action takes place during the wee hours of the morning.

2)   When the Lime line is rising, and then suddenly snaps, the ADX indicator becomes essentially useless, it means price has stalled. But be careful, ADX can be tricky; The Lime line may start to rise again. Once it has reached 70, it has pretty much run its course.

3)   If the Red line or the Blue line are ever on top of the Lime line and both are rising, watch out, it means price is either dropping or rising rapidly. This is always a good indicator that that the market is making a big move when Red or Blue is over the Lime line.

When you have added ADX to each of your templates you are through with this step.

Now comes the most important indicator, the Exponential Moving Average or EMA. I won't get into a lengthy explanation on the difference between the various moving averages, but I will say that the EMA is the most accurate in the short term and works best for our purposes. So once again please go to your Standard M15 template, click on the gold star at the top left of the platform and scroll down the Indicators until you reach Moving Average. Double click on Moving Average and a box will open up in the middle of the screen. I want you to add these moving averages to each template for each chart. You will be adding four different Moving Averages to each template. Below is a table I have made for you to simply add them on, once they are all added I'll explain what they are for, but really it should become quickly obvious what they are for once you have them added and all four time frames are open.

Timeframe M15	Period	MA Method:	Apply to:	Style	Line
Moving Average	9	Exponential	Close	DodgerBlue	Thick
Moving Average	26	Exponential	Open	Magenta	Thick
Moving Average	27	Exponential	Close	DodgerBlue	Dotted line
Moving Average	78	Exponential	Open	Magenta	Dotted line

Timeframe: H1	Period:	MA Method:	Apply to:	Style	Line
Moving Average	9	Exponential	Open	DodgerBlue	Thick
Moving Average	26	Exponential	Close	Magenta	Thick
Moving Average	36	Exponential	Open	DodgerBlue	Dotted line
Moving Average	104	Exponential	Close	Magenta	Dotted line

Timeframe: H4	Period:	MA Method:	Apply to:	Style	Line
Moving Average	9	Exponential	Open	DodgerBlue	Thick
Moving Average	26	Exponential	Close	Magenta	Thick
Moving Average	45	Exponential	Open	DodgerBlue	Dotted line
Moving Average	130	Exponential	Close	Magenta	Dotted line

Timeframe D1	Period	MA Method	Apply to	Style	Line
Moving Average	9	Exponential	Open	DodgerBlue	Thick
Moving Average	26	Exponential	Close	Magenta	Thick
Moving Average	45	Exponential	Open	DodgerBlue	Dotted line
Moving Average	130	Exponential	Close	Magenta	Dotted line

If you applied the Moving Averages to your templates correctly you should now open all four time frames in your platform and attach the proper template to each one. They are as follows:

1)   AUDUSD M15: Standard Template M15

2)   AUDUSD H1:   Standard Template H1

3)   AUDUSD H4:   Standard Template H4

4)   AUDUSD D1:   Standard Template D1

Now the most important part, study each chart and notice how the 9/26 EMA crossover is the standard Moving Average for that chart, it is the thick magenta and dodger blue lines. But look at the dotted magenta and dodger blue lines as well, they match the solid 9/26 EMA's for the time frame preceding it! This is the secret to The Harvest, the dotted lines give you a glimpse into the future of the preceding chart, it's like a crystal ball. When price crosses the dotted magenta line on M15 it means it is also crossing the solid magenta line on H1. This tells you automatically which way the trend is on any particular time frame.

Here is what your new Standard M15 chart should look like:

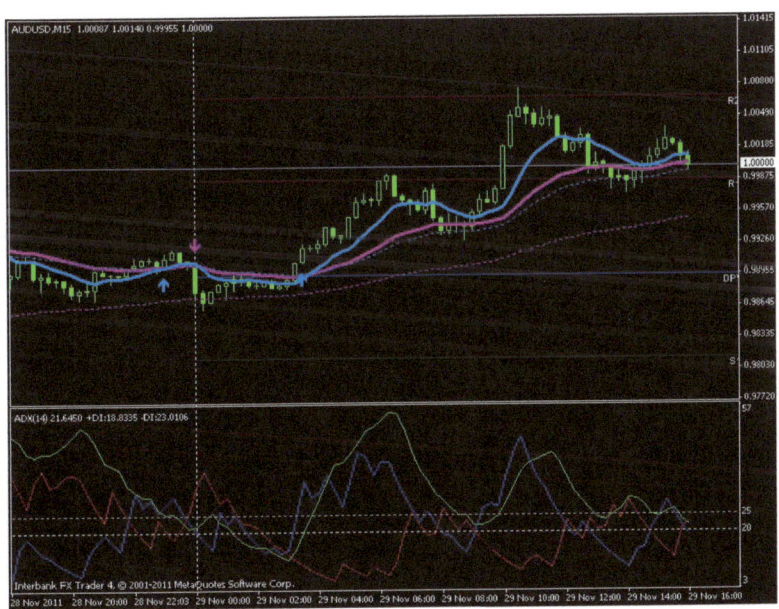

By now it should start to become obvious what we are doing. The M15 chart is a tiny slice of the H1 chart which is a tiny slice of the H4 chart which is a tiny slice of the D1 chart and by looking at the moving averages on the D1 chart we can see what the overall trend is. This brings us to the first rule of The Harvest, never trade against the overall trend!

When trading you should set up each chart separately. This will give you a bird's eye view of price on all four time frames, thus enabling you to know exactly when to enter a trade in direction of the trend. Please note the charts I've shown all contain an arrow where EMA 9 crosses EMA 26 and visa versa, if you would like this indicator please see instructions on how to get it in the Afterword. This indicator will either give a pop alert or an email alert when the two EMA's cross.

The chart also contains another indicator showing lines labeled R1, R2, DPV, S1, S2. These are all support and resistance lines. We'll talk about these later, but again the indicator for these lines are can also be purchased from me for next to nothing, I give instructions how in the Afterword.

Chapter Two: Sewing the Seed

How much seed you want to sew, how much trading capital you want to invest is entirely up to you. For our purposes, in order to make $300 per week, you will need a starting investment of $10000.00. Now I know that is a lot, but as a rule of thumb we can only risk 1.5% of your entire balance per trade. That means a risk/reward ratio of 2:1. We are willing to risk $150 in order to make $300. This is good money management and will keep you in the game for a long time. Remember good trading is not just about profits it's also about capital preservation. Those who go the distance win the most.

Now go back to your broker, whoever you downloaded your MT4 platform from and open an account for $10000.00 at 50:1 leverage. Don't go any higher than this leverage or it will be your downfall. Higher leverage is attractive but it is just as easy to lose big money as it is to make big money using a higher leverage.

I strongly suggest you practice trading for a while using a $10,000 demo account. It's very easy to create such an account, especially using IBFX, just open your platform, click under File and scroll down to Open an Account. Make sure to set it for 10000 USD at 50:1 leverage.

Once you have the account open and fully loaded with the 10K I want you to right click on the chart. Scroll to the first item, Trading and open it up. This is the Market Execution window; it's where you place the trade. Look where is says Volume. I want you to input the number .30. That's what you'll be trading: .30 lots. After this whenever you enter a trade you will trade .30 lots, this mean you can set a fifty pip stop loss and if you lose the trade you will only have lost 1.5% of your capital, or $150.

It also means you are generally shooting for a one hundred pip gain, that's not always possible, sometimes you may only be able to hit the next resistance level. But once we are in a trade I will show you how to move your stop loss to breakeven, then you won't be risking anything at all.

Mind you, if you are unable to open an account for $10,000 you can still open a mini account for say

$1000 or even $100, but you will have to calculate your lot size accordingly, and you will not make the $300 per week as promised. You'll have to build up to a $10,000 account.

At the end of this book I will give you information on how to receive a package of indicators including an excel spreadsheet calculator that will help you keep track of your lot size as you trade. But more on that later.

Chapter Three: Weeding the Crop

Once we have funded our account and determined lot size, now it's time to sort through the various currency pairs looking for a suitable entry. Again, I trade primarily AUDUSD, so I recommend you open a 15 minute AUDUSD chart and apply your Standard M15 template. Depending on the time of day you will see various price movements. If its late afternoon (EST) you are likely to see price moving along at a snail's pace with your moving averages starting to meld together. All of your ADX lines, Lime, Blue and Red are likely to be beneath 20 or 25 indicating that price is ranging, this is generally a dormant time of day when the market is not doing much.

A far better time is to open the chart is around midnight (EST) and anticipate a crossover of your moving averages around 2 to 4 AM when the Frankfurt and then London markets open, this is a high probability trading time and you are very likely to find a trade at this time.

The trade set up we are looking for is very simple. When Moving Average 9 crosses Moving Average 26 (or visa versa) and your Lime ADX line is starting to move above 25, enter the trade at .30 lots. Here is a set up chart to help you locate entries, and weed out the bad trades.

Timeframe: M15	Moving Average	Crosses Moving Average	And ADX Line (Color) crosses 25
Go Long (buy)	9 (dodger blue)	26 (magenta)	Blue and lime
Go short (sell)	26 (magenta)	9 (dodger blue)	Red and lime

Remember, immediately after entering your trade go back to the Market Execution box and set your Stop Loss at fifty pips from your position and your Take Profit 100 pips from your position. You should also make note of any support or resistance levels and plan for price to stall out there. Here is something important to note: you won't always make the whole 100 pips you are looking for on one trade.

Some nights the market will range and not move at all and you may have to wait for the next day for a trading set up. You may make 30 pips the first night, 40 the next et cetera. Always remember, if going long, stay in the trade as long as price stays above the dodger blue (EMA 9) moving average. If in a short trade, stay in the trade as long as price is below the magenta line (EMA 26).

Support and resistance provide the speed bumps along the way, and price may stall out or even retrace a bit, if that happens, get out of the trade and hang on to whatever profit you have. The market isn't going anywhere, you can always come back to fight another day. Your target is 100 pips for the week, it doesn't matter how you break it up, you have five trading days a week to find the right set up, and with our math you will easily make your $300 profit by the end of business Friday.

Chapter Four: Preparing For Harvest

Once your trade is live it is vitally important that you "tend your crop" so to speak. Once I open a trade I always watch to make sure there is no fundamental news announcement to send price out of whack, and I continue to move my stop loss first to the entry price (once you are "in the money" of course) and then even further as profit grows. A live trade is like a budding plant and must be tended until it has fully bloomed.

If you are long, once price closes below the dodger blue line (EMA 9) you are pretty much through, same if you are short, once price closes above the magenta line (EMA 26) the trade has pretty much reached its zenith. You can always check higher time frames to see if there is more wiggle room on the EMA 9 and EMA 26 crossover there; it may be that you are at the very beginning of a trend on a higher time frame, in which case you may want to stay in the trade a bit longer. Other indicators like Fibonacci et cetera can be used to determine exactly where to exit a trade on a higher time frame.

Additionally, you may want to exit partially, taking some of the profit now and let the rest run its course. If that's the case, go back to your market Execution window, and Buy (if you short a position) .15 back. Or Sell (if you are long a position) .15 (or whatever amount you want) back. The rule of thumb is always, "cut your losses short and let your profits run."

Once the trade has run its course, close it out either manually or with a limit order and get out. You did it! $300 a week as promised! If you were only able to make part of the $300, then consider this just a preparation for the final harvest and wait for the next favorable setup. The Forex is a 24 hour, 5 day a week, four trillion dollar a day market, so there is usually a trade set up to be found anywhere at virtually anytime, although 2-6 AM EST, 9-11 AM EST and 7-11 PM EST seems to be the best times to trade.

Chapter Five: The Harvest

The Harvest, for our purposes comes when you have made your $300 for the week. I strongly advise you to stop trading for the week once you have made your goal. If there is a large price move and you make the whole $300 on a Sunday night/Monday morning then congratulate yourself and take the week off. Don't over trade, get greedy trying for more, that's when you start racking up the losses. Remember, capital preservation is what the game is really all about. You must protect the $10,000 at all costs. Use it like an engine to get you where you want to be. Compound your profits and in a few years you could be a millionaire. Its happens a lot more on the Forex than people believe.

The Harvest really is what you want it to be. The strategy I've given you can easily be adapted for higher or lower risk, for greater or smaller profit.

Here are some final rules that may help you along the way:

Don't be greedy; remember "Pigs get fat, hogs get slaughtered."
Don't revenge trade, which is trading right away while still angry after a losing trade.
Don't spread your stops out, leave them right where they are until you can bring them to break even.
Don't cut your trades short, meaning don't just grab a small amount of profit and get out, if it's a good set up, be patient, the trade will develop and pay off in the end.

Afterword

If this book, or the strategy it contains has bothered you in any way, please tell me. I am a relatively new, albeit successful trader myself and I am here to learn and grow. With that in mind I welcome your comments both good and bad. Seriously, if you can help me improve, then I welcome your comments and suggestions.

More importantly, if you have something to share that will improve this trading methodology than by all means let me know, I would really appreciate it and I will be sure to share it with others.

Here's how to contact me by email:

cecilselkirk@gmail.com

or by mail:

29488 Woodward Avenue #352
Royal Oak, MI 48073

I always respond to every email I receive.

Thanks for reading. I look forward to hearing from you. Also, for those who are interested, there is an indicator pack that comes with this system. It includes the ADX crossing 20 alert indicator, a moving average crossover alert signal (these are the arrow signals you shown on the example charts), a price crossing moving average signal, and an excellent spreadsheet calculator developed by a mathematician particularly for position sizing.

To receive the indicators send $3.00 via PayPal to: **tradervic@comcast.net**. Thank you and happy trading!

The Harvest Forex Mentoring Program

The Harvest Forex Mentoring Program is a live, person-to-person mentoring program designed to fit your Forex learning needs. For eight one-hour sessions (or five ninety-minute sessions) author and professional Forex trader Cecil Selkirk will work with you via Skype (voice) and Join.me (to view Cecil's live charts) to help you learn how to trade what has been described as the "toughest" market out there to learn; the four trillion dollar a day foreign currency exchange.

The Harvest Forex Mentoring Program is designed with the beginning trader in mind. During these eight hour sessions Cecil will personally teach you to:

Set up your MT4 trading platform and open a demonstration account

Apply **The Harvest** indicators and templates to your trading platform

Help you to set up live trading signal alerts to your cell phone or home computer

Help you to use **The Harvest** method to successfully trade for the first time

Cover the fundamentals of Forex trading, including; developing a trading plan, key market times, how to execute a trade, setting up stop loss and take profit, understanding the news and economic indicators, drawing trend lines and Fibonacci retracements, and understanding and implementing money management.

Swing trading and scalping

Working with Indicators and Expert Advisors (or "MT4 Trading Robots")

Cecil is ready to work with you on your schedule, regardless of what time zone you live in. So are you ready to get started? The price for **The Harvest Forex Mentoring Program** is just $99 for eight one-hour (or five ninety-minute) sessions made payable through PayPal to: tradervic@comcast.net. After making payment download Skype and join.me (basic) and then contact Cecil at: cecilselkirk@gmail.com. Still not sure? Send your questions about the program to cecilselkirk@gmail.com for a prompt reply.

The Harvest Forex Mentoring Program
"Trade for Need, Not for Greed"

The Harvest Forex MT4 Expert Advisor
(or "Trading Robot")

Too busy to trade? Author and professional Forex trader Cecil Selkirk, in conjunction with award winning mathematician and Metaquotes Language Editor/MQL coding expert Grzegorz Antosiewicz have developed **The Harvest MT4 Expert Advisor** (or "Trading Robot"). Based on **The Harvest** trading principles, **The Harvest MT4 Expert Advisor** is a grid trading system that with the proper settings and money management can grow your account phenomenally. This Expert Advisor, plus a free 60 minute consultation with Cecil can be had for only $299 via PayPal to tradervic@comcast.net.

www.ingramcontent.com/pod-product-compliance
Lightning Source LLC
Chambersburg PA
CBHW041117180526
45172CB00001B/291